AF101669

Common
Sense 2.0

Common Sense 2.0

Exposing the Lies of the Deep State.
Envisioning a Better America.

Mike Porter

PALMETTO
PUBLISHING
Charleston, SC
www.PalmettoPublishing.com

Copyright © 2023 by Mike Porter

All rights reserved.

No portion of this book may be reproduced, stored in a retrieval system, or transmitted in any form by any means–electronic, mechanical, photocopy, recording, or other–except for brief quotations in printed reviews, without prior permission of the author.

Paperback ISBN: 979-8-8229-3111-4

*Special thanks to
Author Samuel Rosette*

*Special thanks to
Duncan Porter*

*Sam has 2 books out and guided me
through the early stages of the process .
Duncan Porter is my father and
teaches me common sense daily.*

INTRODUCTION

In the course of the development of our world, we have seen the rise and fall of civilizations, nations, and cultures. Consequently, the rise and fall of nations is directly related to the turning points that have challenged each nation during its history. The way in which a nation faces its challenges and the turning points in its history are in direct correlation with how long or brief the history of that nation will be. When a nation faces challenges, its leaders must make wise decisions that will preserve and protect the nation and its civilians. If the decisions made by the leaders are not based on common sense, solid evidence, pragmatic logic, and facts, then that nation facess certain failure. Policy decisions based on anything else, such as race, emotion, gender, or appeasement, will most certainly cause that nation to cease to exist due to the failed decisions and policies that it has made. The decisions and policies made by any nation must be made by a large group of decision-makers. Any policy initiated by a nation that is ruled by a single person or small group is doomed to failure.

There are two principles that clearly distinguish a failing nation or civilization. When logic becomes the enemy and truth becomes a menace, the failure of a nation is almost certainly imminent. When citizens of a nation are able to see and discern those two truths occurring, then they will realize that their nation has but a short time to peacefully exist. Their nation is most certainly doomed to civil unrest and failure. Eradicating and correcting the problems is the only way to continue to exist peacefully. Today in the United States, sadly, this is the state of affairs that exists.

THE DEEP STATE

Common sense has told every American on the street for the last one hundred years that politicians are corrupt. They've been peddling influence and laundering money almost since the day America was born. Now the problem is even worse because the deep state's rich, powerful people, who really rule the world, are even more powerful and corrupt because they have untold billions of dollars to play with. And they have the news media and the social media that they've bought and paid for to mold and shape their thoughts and lies in an attempt to brainwash the masses into following their lies. The deep state would like nothing better than to start a new world order in which the masses live in a socialistic-communistic society, relying upon the government to support them and supply them with everything they need. The deep state could then spin the lies any way they wished and basically create a false history of the world utilizing the super-technology they've obtained. They would do as every other communist regime has ever done, destroying the family bond, religious beliefs, and free thinking. In essence, the deep state's goal is to bring about a one-world government, one-world currency, and a one-world religion in which we all worship some all-powerful state that has all the answers. They feed you, clothe you, house you; in essence, they are your *God*. But I don't have to tell most Americans that, because they have suspected this was happening for a generation. And I don't have to tell the average American that the government I have just described to you is communism. It's dressed up to be a socialist utopian paradise where all people of all races will live happily ever after in a new world order. Common sense tells every American that it's ridiculous to think that it will ever happen. But sadly, this is the goal of the deep state. And they have the means and the power to make it happen.

For the last thirty-plus years in politics, this deep state agenda has been inching closer to becoming a reality. They've installed candidates who are socialists. They've openly espoused their intentions. You have your openly outspoken socialists like Bernie Sanders. You have your friendly neighborhood socialist salesmen like Barack Obama. And you have your deep state secret-society socialists. Hillary Clinton is a good example of a closet socialist. Remember her book *It Takes a Village*? The deep state has indoctrinated the young people to believe the big lie. They've also dumbed down the youth with cell phones and computers. Most youth are more focused on playing around on their phones today than they are on learning. If they need to know something, they just look it up on the computer. And it's led American youth to be less motivated than youth from communist countries that force their kids to learn. If their students don't learn the required content, then the "state" sends them to a labor center, where they can be of use to the state. And there's no hope of getting out of that life. And in communist countries, depending on the child's behavior, IQ level, or family history, the youth will be placed wherever the state needs them without regard to the child. The simple fact is that American youth are disinterested in learning. They are *not held accountable* to learn. They can get whatever information they want to get simply by accessing the computer. And another simple fact is that they're not getting the deeper analysis. The narrative is all they ever seem to follow, and it's full of lies and half truths. This is by design. The deep state wants followers, not leaders. So now, in America, a generation later, we have youth who are indoctrinated in school to believe that socialism is just another form of government. That's ridiculous! Tell that to a person who just swam through shark-infested waters to escape socialism! Common sense has shown that time and time again. That's why America spent a century showing people the difference between capitalism and socialism.

People don't leave here to go there. They get on rickety little rafts and float across oceans to come here. It's easy to vote socialism in. However, once you're in it, you have to *fight* your way out! Today, with the deep state's power, it would be nearly impossible. And all the millions of American soldiers who have fought and died for our freedoms would have died for nothing. Freedom would be a thing of the past. Common sense would be a thing of the past.

THE TWILIGHT ZONE?

The World Economic Forum (WEF) met in 2020, and their guest speaker was Xi Jinping from China. Their members are the richest, most elite and powerful rulers of the world—multinational business leaders and other deep state elitists that basically control the world economy. Their stated goal for this meeting was to implement what they call "The Great Reset." It's a one-world global economy in which all world economies function together. *One world economy, one world currency.* They say no one will own anything, but everyone will be happy. Common sense screams at me that it's communism! Somebody's got to own something! This is the insidious plan to make Americans believe the lie and surrender our property and our freedoms! We will end up like every other communist regime, sweating and toiling away while the elite deep state enjoys the socialist utopian paradise. The deep state thought that after COVID, the time was right to implement the Great Reset program. They are making the preparations as we speak! Don't fall for the lie!

And now, we have a situation in America in which the elections have been won by razor-thin margins. Common sense tells us that something's going on. Computerized voting machines have been rigged before. Anyone with common sense knows that! So here we are today, wondering what's going on with our government. We're all looking around and thinking, "Is this real? Or are we living in the Twilight Zone?"

Well, my friends, welcome to the Twilight Zone. It's real, and it's happening. The deep state candidate Joe Biden won, and America is in a fight for it's life and its future. Life, liberty, and the pursuit of happiness are at stake. The deep state has spent the last three years setting up its infrastructure in government to initiate a complex "Great Reset" takeover. They've installed a two-tiered justice system. And they're tearing apart the middle class economically. They're setting up a system in which there will be no way to escape the game. C'mon, man! If Biden is any example of the new world order socialist utopian paradise, then get me the hell away from it! Run away quickly before you become enslaved!

THE TURNING POINT

In 2015, Donald Trump announced his candidacy for President of the United States. Running in the GOP, he entered a large field of candidates vying for that position. His Democratic opponent was Hillary Clinton, former Secretary of State under Barack Obama. Obama's Vice President was Joe Biden. Obama was the first black man to hold the office of President. He ran against rather weak Republican candidates, John McCain and Mitt Romney, and his public relations and media profile won him the election. However, his presidency was one of appeasement. His foreign policy decisions appeased most of the enemy nations of the US. He made many policy decisions by executive decision while convincing Congress to give approval at a later time. Iran, Russia, China, and many other nations hostile to the United States benefited greatly from his decisions. His foreign-policy decisions made our world a much more dangerous place.

His domestic policies were riddled with inflation and rising prices. After eight years of his administration, the citizens were ready for a change. Obama's Secretary of State, Hillary Clinton, wished to continue the socialistic policies Obama initiated. She also had a great public relations campaign and the news media's support. She tried to endear the citizens to elect her as the first woman President of the United States.

Candidate Trump had no political experience. He was a very successful businessman and a very smart, eloquent speaker. He faced a large field of prominent candidates. He ran a shrewd campaign. I, like many Americans, had seen and heard all the career politicians espousing the party lines on both sides of the aisle. However, like many Americans, common sense told me that the endless diatribes by the politicians on both sides of the aisle was nothing but the same mumbo jumbo we had heard for a generation, and electing a career politician would simply lead to the same old political promises broken time and time again. The citizenry longed for an outsider with a fresh approach to making America great again. And Donald Trump was the answer to America's problems. Against heavy pressure even from constituents in the Republican party and extreme pressure from the media and the Democratic party, who invented lies and collusions, Trump went on to win the presidential election and began his term in office. This historic achievement completely upset the dark-state establishment politicians who had been corrupting our political system for decades. Their corruption was becoming exposed, and every day that went by exposed more and more of the graft and corruption. Politicians who were "on the take" could no longer practice their corruption and money laundering without being exposed. Finally, the American economy began running on all cylinders, and the American people were seeing relief. Americans were happy and easily ready to vote for a second term for Trump. The left had been manufacturing lies and false stories of collusion with Russians since 2015, and it never ceased after Trump won the election. The deep state was in severe trouble and had to manufacture an emergency! With the help of the Chinese, a worldwide pandemic was initiated to lower populations and create chaos. These are tools of the deep state, which they utilize when they know nothing else is working. They manufactured lies about how the pandemic started that were laughable. Bats at a wet market? They blamed Trump for closing off the borders, when in reality, he saved millions of American lives. The deep state actually wanted more people to die, reducing the population of deplorables. Eugenics is another tool of the deep state. They would like nothing more than to reduce worldwide populations to a manageable level of around 1 billion. When President Trump's term of office was coming to an end, the economy was in chaos due to the manufactured pandemic, and the deep state thought that this would vanquish their foe. However, surprisingly, the resilient economy Trump had created was bouncing back rapidly, and Americans were proud of the job he had done. Still, though, there was the brainwashed segment of our society that believed the lies of the deep state, and there were elements that actually believed that socialism is what we needed to move forward. I once heard an Obama staffer make the statement that they would like to make America into a "socialist utopian paradise." Those words are a dichotomy. You can't have utopia or a paradise in a socialistic society. Only the bourgeoisie or ruling class would be living in a utopian paradise, while the masses would be fully controlled in a totalitarian society, which would erode and eradicate the freedoms of the American masses. Knowing that it seemed inevitable that Trump would win reelection and expose the deep state's gains and secrets, they devised a sinister plan to rig the elections. Electronic voting machines have been used across the world and actually have a history of being rigged. Italy is an example, where they discovered ballot-rigging after the fact. But let me put forth the question to you. Common sense tells us that where there's a will, there's a way to rig the machines. It just takes a computer geek to enter a code to make every other vote be a vote for the chosen deep state candidate. And most Americans believe that it's possible for our government to do such a thing. And in 2020, the deep state chose Joe Biden to be their candidate! As President Trump was holding political rallies that year with hundreds of thousands of people coming out after COVID to show their support, the deep state candidate was deep in his basement, running a campaign. The deep state knew they couldn't let him out in public much because common sense would have shown the American people how bumbling and inept he was at running a country. Instead, he read scripted dialogues from his basement. On election night, many Americans went to sleep thinking that Trump would inherit a second term. Common sense told us that would probably be the outcome. But mysteriously, duffel bags of votes sitting on the floor below vote counters somehow magically turned the tide, and the deep state candidate Joe Biden was elected. Many common-sense Americans were outraged and actually went to Washington, D.C., to protest. But the deep state sent their undercover people in to incite even more violence. And the so called "insurrection" was born on January 6, 2021. Naturally, the deep state blamed Trump for this, and he was labeled a traitor to the nation. The bought-and-paid-for media hyped the story and convinced many Americans of their opinion. The media refused to investigate both sides of the story. Common sense also tells us that any nation with a one-sided media outlet is doomed to failure. Case in point: the TASS news agency of the old USSR. So on January 20, 2021, Joe Biden was sworn into office, vowing to eradicate all the failed policies of the previous administration. Common sense told us that most of those policies were not failed policies. When gas prices doubled virtually overnight after the closing of the Keystone XL oil pipeline, was that common sense? When Biden mandated electric cars but conveniently left out Tesla, the leading electric car manufacturer, from the table, was that common sense? Was it common sense to build electric cars but not have the charging-station infrastructure in place? Was it common sense to leave the border wall unfinished, allowing millions of illegal immigrants to flood our borders? Was it common sense to auction off the remaining border wall material at pennies on the dollar? Is it common sense to have an app that allows illegal immigrants to book a free flight to America? Is it common sense not to tell the American people, who are paying for those flights? Is it common sense to give away free crack pipes in vending machines to crackheads? Is it common sense to label parents as domestic terrorists for questioning what is being indoctrinated in their children in public schools? Is it common sense to allow criminals to rampage through stores, shoplifting, and not prosecute them? When the store owner beats or kills a criminal in his store, is it common sense to prosecute the store owner? Is it common sense to defund police and leave the public vulnerable? Is it common sense to allow transgender males to compete in women's sports or use bathroom facilities for women? Is it common sense to allow dangerous drugs like fentanyl to flow across our borders? Is it common sense to appease China while Taiwan relies on our support? Is it common sense to allow senators to spew anti-Semitic rhetoric on the floors of Congress? Is it common sense to constantly allow the DOJ to weaponize against Trump while slow-walking or ignoring other cases that are more important? Is it common sense to allow your crackhead son to get a slap on the hand for tax evasion while other Americans are in prison for the same crimes? Is it common sense to appoint a gender-and-race-based press secretary who can't answer questions? Is it common sense to appoint cabinet positions based on race, gender, or radical-left beliefs? Is it common sense to avoid a press conference to the American people? Is it common sense to continue telling the tall tales about your life, knowing that after fact-checking the information, it turns out to be false? Is it common sense to run up trillions of dollars of debt for ridiculous initiatives that are not proven to work? Is there anything this administration has done that can be labeled as common sense? Was it common sense to be sitting on the beach in Delaware while the people of Maui were burning?

Here's a brilliant example of common sense. When Texas Governor Greg Abbott was getting millions of illegal immigrants crossing his border, he decided to ship them to sanctuary cities that claimed they wanted them. Now they have hundreds of thousands of immigrants in New York, Chicago, Los Angeles, D.C., and other sanctuary cities. And it's funny when their radical leftist mayors go on television and say not to send anymore immigrants. It's kind of like the comical meme I saw where an alien comes to Earth and says, "Take me to your leader." And then it has a picture of Biden hugging the alien and whispering in his ear. The alien then says, "Wait a minute, hold up. Take me back to my ship!" This, sadly, is our current state of affairs.

The current leader of America, President Joe Biden, has filled most if not all of his cabinet and executive positions with people who have only minimal skills. They were put in positions because of race or gender identity or because their leftist beliefs fit the requirements of the "dark powers" who have brainwashed them into believing the lies. I'm not opposed to any person of any race holding an office in government. But they must be fair and balanced. And they must have the qualifications to successfully execute the job. There are multitudes of fair, unbiased Americans of all ethnicities that could successfully perform the jobs. The administration's record of achievement thus far has been minimal to none. The judicial appointments selected have all had one thing in common. Their views on caseloads are all skewed far to the left, bordering on radical and socialistic ideology, which goes against the job description of being fair and unbiased. The arguments they use to comment on why they ruled the way they did are always illogical and contrary to the truth as a normal, logical-thinking American perceives truth. Overall, the entire administration has proven to be the most radical leftist administration in our history, filled with radical elements who wish to usher in a socialistic form of government that will severely limit the freedoms of the civilian population. This has been tried before, in American history and throughout the world, and has been unsuccessful. I will elaborate more later on the dangers of socialism. This administration has also utilized the media and big tech companies to perpetrate lies and half truths in an effort to mislead the public. Remember President Eisenhower's farewell address in 1960, in which he warned Americans to beware of the military-industrial complex linking up. This has clearly been allowed to happen. Case in point: during the last election cycles, many Americans had their social media accounts shut down because they said things that were contrary to the deep state's views. They were free-speech statements that were dangerous to the deep state. Another case in point: when Canadian truckers protested vaccine mandates, the metadata architects shut down their GoFundMe pages as well as the truckers' bank accounts. Common sense tells us that if they have the power to do that, then there is very little a civilian can do to counter that power. When nations do that to its citizens, then we are on the brink of having a totalitarian regime.

This administration has also made alliances with nations that are hostile or unfriendly to the US, Israel, and other allies. This administration has also used principles of racism and tribalism to create a racial divide between whites and all other racial groups. This is part of what they call "woke culture." It's actually a very effective brainwashing ideology that is based on tribalism and untruths. The media elements and their Big Tech allies have pushed this ideology and targeted youth to garner support and more effective use of this maligned ideology. All these tactics and the ideology behind their policies have been tried before, in other countries, and have failed. Radicalism has been encouraged and tolerated while the normal, logical citizenry has suffered loss of property and even loss of life. In total, this country is suffering from multiple problems on multiple fronts. Many of these problems could easily be eradicated by merely enforcing the existing laws governing these problems. Common sense.

THE BUDDY SYSTEM

Now that I've identified the myriad of problems we are facing, let us analyze the problems. I will offer facts and proof of my claims.

President Biden has been a career politician for fifty years. He has always supported socialistic policies and programs designed to promote the minority-based populations of this country.

Tax-and-spend policies and other policies designed to promote minorities and limit the majority population are the standard operating procedures this country has been functioning under for literally one hundred years. They are failed policies designed to slowly eradicate freedoms and brainwash the cultural beliefs of the society.

Biden's cabinet appointments were all based on race, gender, or radical leftist ideology. I am not opposed to officeholders being of different ethnicities, but the officeholders must have the skill set to perform the job adequately and be fair and unbiased. There are adequate numbers of qualified candidates in America of all ethnicities that have the skills necessary to do great things for this country. Unfortunately, Biden appears to have appointed people that lacked the skills necessary for success in their positions. Common sense tells me that he appointed people to whom he owed favors or whose viewpoints were skewed far to the radical left. You must be fair and unbiased when you hold an important position, such as a cabinet position. You are representing all the people, not just the radical left. And when you explain your decisions, they must sound logical to all the people. *Not word salad!* Common sense tells us that this hasn't been the case thus far. Most of the administrative decisions we've seen are totally illogical.

Vice President Kamala Harris was selected by Mr. Biden based solely on her racial profile. She has minimal qualifications for the job and has yet to accomplish even a single task she has been given. Her speeches are totally illogical and make no sense to the vast majority of Americans. Other countries are completely baffled by her word salads and her silly cackling.

Transportation Secretary Pete Buttigieg was a gender-based appointment. As transportation secretary, he has yet to accomplish any significant improvements in the transportation systems across America. But Pete and his husband did have a baby. Adopted, of course.

Press Secretary Karine Jean-Pierre is a gender-and-race-based appointment who by all accounts is ill-equipped for her position. The daily press briefing is comic relief for most Americans. But she claims she is "making history." Comedians everywhere agree!

Secretary of the Treasury Janet Yellen was previously the Federal Reserve Chairman. She hasn't accomplished anything to ease the burden most Americans are facing. They've raised the interest rate to 5 percent to head off inflation, but it doesn't seem to help. Her advanced age and her lack of experience in the field of foreign affairs has been adequately demonstrated, as we have yet to make any achievements in foreign affairs. Recently, on her visit to

China, she actually bowed to the leader, demonstrating the position of weakness we are in across the globe. It was puzzling why the Secretary of the Treasury would travel to China, rather than the Secretary of State.

Secretary of State Antony Blinken has proven so ineffective at his job that many countries will not even host him for a visit. If they do host him, it's always someone of a much lower position that meets with him, and no significant policies or progress has been made in this administration. Rather, the opposite has happened.

Secretary of Homeland Security Alejandro Mayorkas was also a race-based appointment. Thus far, his record on border security has been abysmal. More illegal immigrants have crossed the US border than at any other time in US history. Many of our cities across America are overridden with illegal immigrants who have put an incredible burden on our country's economy. Housing, feeding, and providing for the illegal immigrants has been a nightmare scenario for many major US cities across the country.

Secretary of Housing and Urban Development Marcia Fudge was also a race-based appointment who could actually accomplish great things. She has the skills necessary to accomplish the task. However, the administration has made her job untenable. She has yet to make any significant improvements. Rather the opposite. The millions of illegal immigrants that have crossed into America have turned her job into a nightmare scenario. Housing and feeding these immigrants is akin to welcoming refugees from a war-torn country. It's literally costing America billions of dollars.

Secretary of Energy Jennifer Granholm has had very little effect, if any, on our energy crisis. Respectfully, she has been given an impossible task. President Biden closed down the Keystone XL pipeline on day one of his administration. America's gas prices doubled, and our supply must now be imported. The administration's focus on electric vehicles has proven to be a mixed bag. Lack of charging infrastructure across the country and a radical view of climate change have destined their policies to fail. Americans have suffered the most. Costs have increased across the board on products, and the supply and demand are lagging. As a senator recently said in Congress, "There are no electric dump trucks." This explains the government's excessively fanatical fascination with electric vehicles, their hatred of fossil fuels, and their fanatical, misguided assessment of the climate change issue. Science, in fact, has the answers; however, they skew the science to fit the radical narrative.

However, Secretary Granholm's fascination with electric vehicles hasn't been a complete waste. It was recently revealed that she had not sold all her stock in the company Proterra until three months after her appointment as Secretary of Energy. I wonder how much money she made unethically. Common sense tells us she made a pretty penny in the stock market.

The Secretary of Education is Miguel Cardona. He was also chosen because of race. Since he has taken office, the policies made in the area of education read much like a sci-fi novel. Students are allowed to change their gender identity without parental consent. Gender-changing medical procedures have been made in some instances. When parents react against the policies, they are branded by the FBI as domestic terrorists and put in a national database. This is akin to science-fiction future scenarios where "the state" controls the children, and parents have very little say in the matter.

Other cabinet secretaries and staff positions are equally yoked to ineffective leaders who are basically spewing out the diatribe of the party line. Common sense has left the building!

UNITED WE STAND, DIVIDED WE FALL

The United States are definitely not united. This is obvious to all logical-minded Americans with common sense. What is also clear to the logical-minded citizenry is the vast number of Americans who have been brainwashed by the "dark state" leftist ideology. Clearly, America has divided into two distinct tribes! The reds and the blues are the names I will call them. It sounds like an episode of the television show *Survivor*: two distinct tribes battling for control over the resources. And on a humorous note, it's always the blue tribe that becomes enraged when the red tribe doesn't want to think or act like them. They literally flip out and lose their minds over the fact that red tribe people don't want to be like the blue tribe. Whereas red tribe people could care less about blue tribe. As long as blue tribe mentality doesn't infringe on red tribe territory or red tribe daily life, the red tribe is perfectly fine with allowing the blue tribe to do whatever they want to do in their territory. Common sense tells us that any tribe, culture, or belief structure that feels the need to impose its beliefs and policies on another culture is doomed to failure. Blue tribe mentality is doomed to fail. It's laughable nonsense.

CIVIL WAR?

This tribalism will inevitably lead to civil war. And it is playing out before our very eyes. America is on the brink of civil war! And the "dark state" powers are actually pushing for this to happen. They would like for this to happen so they can further brainwash the citizenry into believing the woke lie. This would give them the power to make executive decisions to use force against the population and further eradicate the rights of the citizens to rebel against the government, thus effectively solidifying their ultimate power over their citizenry and reducing the country to nothing more than another totalitarian regime. Authoritarianism is the goal. The "state" controls all. It would control every aspect of our lives. Where we work, what we eat, where we can travel, what we can say. In essence, what we can think! Brainwashed to follow the rules of the "state." Thinking outside the box would become a crime. Free speech would land you in jail. Guns would be confiscated. Citizens would have no rights and no powers to effectively rebel against authoritarian control.

Sadly, this is where we are if we elect the deep state candidate in 2024. This doesn't mean civil war is imminent; it just means that we are moving toward it. The first Civil War took twenty years to develop into actual warfare. The deep state knows that. And they know that militarily, they would lose the battle. Anyone with common sense can show you the map of blue states and red states and clearly show the overwhelming tactical advantages the red states would possess in an all-out war scenario. That's why the deep state plans are always more insidious. They work slowly and methodically, trying to influence public opinion first. Then, if necessary, they stage an emergency situation to expedite the changes. We will see how it plays out if the deep state candidate is elected. But any deep state scenario that plays out will lack one essential thing… common sense!

WHAT IT IS IS…

No matter who wins the next presidential election, in 2024, common sense screams out to all Americans, there *will be* various forms of violence in America. And you will hear the various media voices and pundits on both sides of the aisle spewing out rhetoric that begins with wording like:

> What it is is…
> What it was was…
> What the deal is is…
> What the real deal was is…
> This type of rhetoric will abound.

Every point that a news media outlet will try to make will include some form of that preface to their point! And if a conservative candidate is elected, be it Trump or another Republican conservative candidate, the left will lose their ever-loving minds and be protesting in the streets and inciting violence. The right will have no choice but to take action to quell the violence. It will make the "summer of love" look like what they called it, a "summer of love." 2025 will be the most violent year in our nation's history. No matter who wins! People with common sense are probably going to need to make preparations for this inevitable scenario. The left will simply not allow sanity to return to America. They've come too far now to allow their political gains to be vanquished. The deep state elitists will fund them to no end. The deep state money and power will continuously create riot after riot as they sit back and comfortably watch the show, laughing and joking about how they have the power to make their brainwashed minions loot, kill, and destroy America. It's the ultimate turn-on to their egos. Will any of their minions ever be invited to dinner with them? Common sense tells me no! Elitists are the type people who like to watch the spectacle of violence, much like the ancient Roman elites would attend the coliseum to watch Christians being torn to bits by hungry lions. It gives them an adrenaline rush. Elitists are the same people that would secretly sneak to Epstein Island to have sex with underage or very young women who were virtual sex slaves, trapped there. It's a mentality that is perverse and addictive. Once trapped in the addiction, it's hard to break free. Much like all addictions. Common sense tells us that if the government wanted to stop the flow of drugs across our borders, they could have easily done it fifty years ago. But they don't want to stop the flow, because it helps them in their ultimate cause to dumb down and degrade the masses. It makes them easier to control. It's another form of slavery.

If the deep state candidate wins the next election, then it's basically over for America. The left will have four more years to build the infrastructure necessary to accomplish the socialist takeover of America. Violence will still happen, but it won't be funded by the elite deep state. And most common-sense Americans living in a blue-tribe state will simply cut their losses and escape to a red-tribe area. This is already happening on a significant level. If a Democrat gets elected next cycle, you can also expect Texas to begin the secession process. Once they begin the process, other states will begin. This will alarm the elitist deep state, and then you can be expecting an event such as a world war or mass pandemic—some event in which millions of people will die. That would be a last-ditch effort to try to hold the fragile union together, blaming all our problems on another country or entity. Whatever scenario the deep state dreams up, one thing will definitely happen: the rights of Americans will be suspended at some point. When that happens, it's almost certain that those rights will never return. Common sense has already told us that throughout our past history. You can vote in socialism easily. But you have to *fight* your way out of socialism!

MY GOD, MY GOD, WHAT HAVE I DONE?

Thirty years from now, all the young people of today will wake up from their drug-induced comas like a bunch of Rip Van Winkles and utter the words, "My God, my God, what have I done?" The deep state government will be in place, and the name of the country will change to the Democratic Socialist Republic of the United States of America! And the former youth of America, who had lauded and cheered how it was because of them that the US "woke up" and because of them a new world order came about. And because of them that history was changed. And they thought of themselves as wise men who saved the world! But in reality, they were the ungodly generation that had brought about their own doom.

And the charade will be allowed to go on for a short time. Just long enough for the Democratic Socialist Republic of the United States of America to get the new artificial intelligence infrastructure in place. Then the fun begins. That's when all Americans' rights and privileges will be stripped from them as they become enslaved by the system. And that will happen virtually worldwide.

And the 90 percent proletariat population will be turned into a slave class, sweating and toiling away for the ruling class, exactly how it is today under communism. And the police force will be AI robots. When a human gets out of line, AI robots will be sent in first to solve the problems. And if there are a few guns left over from before the takeover, those weapons will be ineffective against the AI robots. And as time passes, the future youth will become accustomed to this system of life. The old people who remember the time before will die off, and the New World Order will become the ultimate power over all people.

When AI becomes powerful enough to rule the masses, they will become what is known in the Christian Bible as the "image of the beast." They will cause all people to worship the "state" and what it represents.

By this time, the young people who started the process and thought to themselves how wise and great they were will be old and decrepit—what few are left. And nightly they shall bow down and pray to their invisible God, and they will utter useless babbling to God because they did not understand the truth. Common sense will be a valuable commodity in those days. Even common sense will become a thing of the past.

THE LIGHT AT THE END OF THE TUNNEL

As General Westmoreland once said during the Vietnam War, "We can see the light at the end of the tunnel." Sadly, that never came to fruition. America was entrenched in a quagmire, and the US could not win over the minds of the Vietnamese people. America does still have hope. If we stand strong together, we shall overcome this plight. The next election will determine if our country endures as a free nation or becomes a socialist nation. With roughly a year before the next election, America still has some surprises that could preserve our freedoms and our form of government. Before identifying our surprises, I would like to elaborate further on the weaknesses of the deep state mentality. When George H.W. Bush was campaigning for his second term of the presidency, he once came out of his deep state elitist bunker to venture into the public view. He thought that this would endear him to the people. He ventured to the friendly neighborhood grocery store. And he had so much fun playing with the product scanner. He admired how American technology was advancing and how this new technology would help Americans in their daily lives. He did not realize how ridiculous he looked. Product scanners had already been out for years. The impression this left on the American public was that he was so out of touch with what regular Americans dealt with on a daily basis. Consequently, he lost the election. But he did show Americans how out of touch with reality the deep state elitists were. I guess servants always bought the groceries at his house. This is typical of the elitist mentality. They live in a dreamworld, woefully out of touch with the masses. The light at the end of the tunnel for America will not come from the elitist deep state's sovereign rulers of the world. Common sense tells us that.

SURPRISE, SURPRISE

From the day Biden took office, his administration has held a deep fascination with Donald Trump. He has been ridiculed publicly and punished by trial after trial after trial. They blame this one man for all the world's problems. He's been accused of more ridiculous things than any man in history. Democrats are intensely focused on his every word, his every move, literally every fiber of his being! The man can't make a move without a Democrat questioning why he moved. They call him racist? They call him a traitor? They call him every foul, vulgar, heinous thing imaginable to man. They blame him for COVID? They blame him for riots? They even blame him for climate change? He's almost as bad as Corn Pop, and we all know that "Corn Pop was a bad dude." The elitists have thrown him under the bus so many times that he should have wheel marks all over his body. They have done to him every imaginable thing they could do to destroy the man. Yet he remains stoic. It's admirable how he still remains dignified and respectable. He maintains his self-dignity as well as any man can. He reminds me of the old blues song by Muddy Waters called "Mannish Boy." It's a song about self-dignity as only the legendary

Muddy Waters could portray it. Anyone who knows that song can see the point I'm making. "I'm a man…I'm a full-grown man," as the song implies. Trump's dignity in the face of adversity is a lesson to every man of every ethnicity. And the obvious lesson is that everything the deep state elitists have done to him has only made him stronger as a man. It's obvious to all people with common sense. Elitists, however, lack common sense. Surprise, surprise!

THE SECRET REVOLUTION OF 2024

There is a revolution brewing. It's a grassroots revolution that has begun. You won't hear about it on CNN. You won't hear about it on MSNBC. The one-sided media is clueless about it. But it is the greatest revolution in American history, and it's happening now. This revolution will be talked about by your grandchildren. It will make America the greatest nation in the world and will be talked about forever. It will cross all races and ethnicities and will bring America to that great day we've been singing about since the '60s. And the architects of this revolution will be known as great Americans forever. Their names will be too numerous to mention, but their one deed will live for eternity and will be known as the day America became one nation under God. These brave men and women will make their mark in American history by performing one simple deed. They will come from all walks of life. They will come from all ethnicities. Yet they will change the course of American history and fulfill the dream of a mighty American from the last generation. They will break the chains of bondage, and America will reach the promised land. This revolution is happening now. Black men and black women are breaking the shackles that bound them to the Democratic party. That evil party that birthed the KKK. The party that created Jim Crow laws. The party that has promised to help blacks and other ethnicities for generations, only for them to see tiny drops of water trickling down. It's time to live the dream set forth by Dr. Martin Luther King Jr. Black men and women across this nation and all men and women are waking up and voting for Trump. They're voting Republican. The party of Lincoln. They've seen what this country has done to one man and can sympathize with his suffering. We've seen the persecution Trump has had to endure, and we can relate to it! Because it's our struggle! We've fought that struggle for hundreds of years! It's a struggle we are familiar with. And finally, it's time to break the shackles of the Democratic party. Our votes cast for Trump will break the cycle of suffering and create a new, free America where we can live out our dreams, where people are no longer judged by the color of their skin but by the content of their character. And the old-guard elitist Democrats will no longer have control over the black race or any other race. They will fade away and be cast down. Men of all colors will stand strong together and fight for freedom. Common sense will once again rule this nation, and we will be one. We must stand together for freedom!

THERE'S A FORK IN THE ROAD. WHICH WAY DO WE GO?

America stands on the brink of eternity! What I mean is this: This country has always been the beacon of freedom for the entire planet! Our multicultural diversity has given us a power that no other nation in history has had or probably ever will have. We've enjoyed the best lifestyle of any nation because of our multicultural diversity. We pick the best parts of each culture, of each race, and we celebrate those traits as our own. Black men, Hispanic men, White men, Asian men, Native American men, Pacific Islander men, mixed race men—in essence, all men and women of our great nation have made great contributions to this country and moved this nation forward to become the greatest nation the world has ever known. And it's time for America to live out the creed set forth by Dr. Martin Luther King Jr. Let's meet at the table of brotherhood and agree that the free capitalist republic that was created by great men, set forth long ago, is our strength. And multicultural diversity is our strength. We are not a socialist nation! We may have picked the best parts of socialism and made them our own. But that's what a multicultural free society does. We take the best parts of all things and make them American. The world sees it. They risk life and limb to claw their way here to become a part of this land of opportunity. We must *wake up*! We must preserve and protect democracy. We can't risk losing our freedom to the deep state Democrat machine that would love to shackle us as wage slaves, toiling away in a totalitarian government that controls everything we say and do.

If you ever saw the movie *The Hunger Games*, you will see that we are living in pre-*Hunger Games* conditions. The freakos living in the cities lived luxuriously, while 90 percent of the population sweated, toiled, and labored under the brutal taskmasters to pay for their lifestyle. Common sense tells us that we "ain't gonna be" the 10 percent living in luxury! I can't take that chance, and you shouldn't either. And I'm definitely not going to participate in any gladiator games to give deep state Democrat freakos their sadistic pleasure! I've worked too hard in my life to be put in a farm labor camp, shoveling hog manure for some purple-haired freako dining on pork tenderloin and caviar!

As for me, I'm taking the *right fork in the road*. I'm voting *Republican*. I'm voting for *Trump*! I'm going to break these shackles that have bound me to the Democrats! I've got nothing to lose but everything to gain. I choose freedom! I'm urging my fellow brothers and sisters of all colors to join with me! And we can join together at the table of brotherhood and sing the words:

> *Free at last*
> *Free at last*
> *Thank God Almighty*
> *We are free at last!*

ABOUT THE AUTHOR

Mike Porter hails from the great state of Texas where he raises livestock on a modest ranch. He holds a B.M.E and a B.A. from West Texas A&M University. He's been a defense contract worker, professional musician, history teacher, and transportation logistics manager.

Common Sense 2.0 is his first literary work. It is an expose of the current state of political affairs in America. It also gives shocking insight to where the USA is heading and provides possible future scenarios based on the dangers we currently face.

www.ingramcontent.com/pod-product-compliance
Lightning Source LLC
LaVergne TN
LVHW041716060526
838201LV00043B/772